A LITTLE

In life we are blessed to have Mama
She is the matriarch of the family because when
daddy's gone it's her alone that have to raise her
family.

She's the one to toil and labour and keep the
family going. Hence Mama alone gives us
strength and wise teachings to carry on in life.

She never leaves us
She does all she can to make her children and
family happy.

She is Mother and Father, hence she is the
Womb and Cradle of Life – Good Life.

She is Nubian hence she is Mama Africa
She is Woman – the Womb of Good God.

Michelle Jean

Mama you alone and as you pray for your children and provide for them, I am proud of you; proud to call you Mama – My Nubian and Africa Queen.

You never left us to die but sacrificed so much for us including your life and happiness.

You are our Black Mother as well as our blessing from God – Good God.

You are God sent
Our strength and Hope – more than Faith and Belief, you are our True and Good Life.

Michelle Jean

You know what Good God, I am not going to cry. I'm just going to bare my burdens alone because I am all alone.

All I can do is write and complain to you about the troubles I am facing with my children. The problems and troubles that face me in life.

Like I said, I cannot complain to you anymore because you are no help to me hence I feel I am on the losing side when it comes to you. I know I am wrong but this is my thought because the problems are coming hence my dreams of me being naked and in the streets.

You know what Good God, I cannot go through anymore stress and heartache at the hands of my children anymore.

I need a clean life but it cannot be because of my son.

I need relief
I need safety
I need sanity
I need rescuing but you have failed me.

When it comes to my children you have failed me.

My second son has put my life – my household in jeopardy and it's like you don't care. You don't give a damn.

You're not standing up for me nor are you opening up your mouth to tell me what to do.

I tell you everything but what the hell is the point when you can't do a damn thing to help me.

God – Good God what is wrong with my son? God what did I do to deserve this. I've been through too much in my life for my son to do this to me. Yes I kicked him out before and that didn't last because he's back in my house.

I've struggled too long with my children raising them on my own for my son to do this to me.

Please tell me what horrible sin I've committed – done for you to hate me so much that my son had to do this to me?

I've tried my best until I've gotten sick and in my sick state, I am still facing trials and tribulations at the hands of my own – children.

I have no fight left in me
I can't anymore

I truly have to let go because to me at this moment and time, life isn't worth it and if suicide was not a grave sin, I would have ended my life already. I have pickney trouble, spiritual troubles, trouble all around.

I've been disrespected so much by some of them – my children that I truly want to walk away from them but I have to endure it all until they come of age when I can leave.

You know what God let me leave my heartache and pain alone because who feels it knows it.

I can't call his father because he's a sperm donor. A father in name only and to the way things are, I truly wished I never gave them his name. I am the one raising my children hence they should have nothing of his, not even is corrupted and slimy DNA.

Like I said, I can't call him because I know he would not help. I've asked him for help before and he could not help. My phone calls went unanswered hence I am on my own.

Like I said, as single mothers we have to bare the burn and pain alone and these kids don't see this. All they see is self hence some say if daddy was there they wouldn't do this or do that. That's a bleeping cop out to me because my daddy wasn't there for the important years of my life. It was Mama alone and she drilled education in our heads. When he did end up in our lives....well you know how that turned out.

Hence I dedicate Mama Alone by I-Octane to all the single mothers and fathers including grandparents out there.

Instead of these kids holding their heads high and say let me be somebody, they add to your stress and pain and cause you more pain – shame. Hence I can't do this anymore.

Good God I can't. I am defeated – truly defeated. There's no hole for me to crawl into hence I' m done. I have to be done with you and them and all that I do.

I can't walk alone anymore. I truly can't because I truly don't know what I've done that is so vile and despicable to deserve this. Yes it's my son's life but I so wanted and needed goodness for all my children. I know I cannot blame you because you did not lay with me and get them. I can only blame me for not asking you for good and clean children. Children that don't lie or deceive – do wrong to be in the wrong circle – crowd. I am the one to blame because I picked up garbage from the bottom of the barrel – in this case the bottomless pit and gave him life when he was undeserving of it.

Like I said God, I can't anymore hence I hope she that is to come will do a better job than me.

Michelle Jean
December 08, 2013

God no one knows how much we cry
No one knows our prayer and tears on the toilet
seat – bowl.

No one knows the heartache and pain that we
feel; the feeling of abandonment by our
children's father's and by you Good God.

Many see us but they don't see the darkness
that surrounds us inside and outside.

They don't know, they truly do not know.

Trust me I want to give up – need to give up. I
am mother hence I have to live. I have to push
on and where I end up I end up despite my
struggles and pain. I gave birth to my children
hence I cannot abandon them but yet I truly
want and need to because of my pain –
struggles, hurt and pain.

Michelle Jean

God it's not about you but about me today. I can't deal with the hardships and pain of raising my children anymore.

They don't listen hence I've failed as a mother and father.

I am no good to you. If my children does not listen and respect me, how will others respect and listen to me?

My second son's friends have disrespected my home and me because of him and I can't go through anymore. I truly can't deal with anymore disrespect anymore. It's like I have no talk in my own home. Mi a di gyal well no more.

I have to sort my life out and let the chips fall where they may. I know I am not the only one feeling pain but on this day, let it be about me and me alone.

Enough is enough when it comes to my niceness. You cannot hang on to children that constantly put your life in jeopardy.

I've come too far to let my children put me behind bars for their wrongs. *This kid – child does not listen.* His friends are his keep so let them continue to lead him down the precipit of hell. He will get there. It's just a matter of time because he does not listen. His friends are whom he's giving up his future for and I give you my word, I will not be there for him because I am tired of talking to him. It's not like I don't see certain things and tell him. I do but he constantly defends his friends. So in the end I hope they will be there for him because I won't be. Mi dream too much and si too much but a so.

Let him continue to ruin his life for them because on that day, you have my infinite and indefinite word of truth that I will disinherit him without any guilt or remorse because he does not bleeping listen. Trust me I will petition you to take his name out of your book of life if you haven't already done so.

There is only so much I can bare and I cannot bare anymore hence I give up on him and you. I truly can't do this anymore. I cannot live amongst deceitful and dishonest children. I am trying but I am losing the war and battle when it comes to my children and myself. I truly can't anymore hence I need to find the true me without reliance on you.

Michelle Jean
December 08, 2013

God I am tired
When does it become easier as a parent?

At what age do we throw in the towel and say no more?

Why do I even bother?
Why do I even say it's good to do good when all you get in return is heartache and pain?

Why do I even talk about true love when my children only love, think true love and love is the same?

Oh man why couldn't I have understood the memo you sent out hence I say you are a lousy teacher but great – an excellent protector.

You protect me but you do not give me child rearing advice. Wow I am so feeling it right now.

I can't get angry I just have to stay calm. I can't lose my head lest I destroy everything in this apartment.

I have to write and keep my blood pressure down.

I have to be real because if my temper flairs, I would probably demolish this apartment if not rip it apart brick by brick.

I can't allow myself to swear because if I do hell would not be able to contain me. I would beat the crap out of everyone in hell including Death and Satan and then go looking for more to beat the crap out of.

I have to keep my head because the Jamaican in me want to come out hence I will restrain myself from the brutal anger within. I have to lean on me because I truly cannot lean on you hence I have to write to get my anger and frustrations out in my little way.

Michelle Jean
December 08, 2013

I know the pain of raising my children alone.

I know the sacrifices
My heartache
Grief

My road is not easy hence at times I ask why me?

Why did I have to choose and chose you Good God?

Why did I have to walk your lonely and painful road?

I see others and how they are happy, enjoying life but yet I am confined to hell feeling pain.

I know others are feeling it too, even worse than me but I can't take anymore. I can't go through any more heartache and pain, nor can I think of them on this day.

I cannot take the stress of it all anymore. In all that I have done to secure the well being of my family I've ended up failing, even want to end my own life.

I've pleaded with you God – Good God about this and all I've gotten from you is nothing. All I've gotten at times is more pain.

How can I live for you when I can't even live for me anymore?

I am tired
Tired of it all

I cannot hold onto a god that cannot truly hold on to me.

My road is rough and tuff and I can't go through anymore.

I truly can't. Good God, I just don't want the stress anymore. I truly don't need it but I have to face it. I have to keep on moving though I have given up.

I truly need to recharge because I truly do not know where my head is at right now.

Michelle Jean
December 08, 2013

You know God – Good God Genesis was not wrong when it said woman had to bare the pain of child birth.

We give birth to our children. And as woman; billions of us not hundreds of millions of us; we are the ones raising our children alone.

We are single parents because the men high tail it. Abandon us to raise our children alone.

Tell me something Good God. How is this fair to us?

Where's the family unit?
Where are our family values – priorities?

I see the fighting and the squabbling of some parents over child support and I have to say really.

When did children become the pawns of parents?

When did a child say pick me before they were born?

When did money become valuable and children become valueless in the eyes and sight of their parents?

Truly tell me something Good God. Is a home a true home without a mother and father?

I have to ask Good God because I never wanted to raise my children alone but I have to. I have to endure the pain hence I ask again. Is a home a true home without a mother and father?

As single parents some of us put so much into raising our children the right way but because of company – friends, some of our children choose and chose the wrong path.

Ah God, I complain to you so much and you are going through the same things but on a much larger – grander scale.

How selfish am I because in all I have done so far, I have not considered your pain or even considered just how busy you might be.

As usual I am only thing of me and not of your problems as well.

You have trouble too because you have to contend with me and all of humanities problems and heartache.

It's a wonder you haven't told me to take a number and shut the hell up because I am the least of your worries right now.

It's a wonder you haven't told me you have other more important priorities apart from me.

Oh well hopefully things will work out in a good way for me because despite me giving up, I know you are still my keep.

You are there with me.

Michelle Jean

God I've tried and like I said, I can't try with my kids anymore.

I cannot uphold the slackness anymore.

I can't do it.

I cannot allow my son to or any of my children to jeopardize my well being anymore.

I need to live and when you cannot do that with your children or around your children then something is definitely wrong.

I cannot endanger my life anymore because of them.

I need to grow now as well as truly stop complaining because I am truly getting fed up of complaining to you.

I need to be free of the hindrances in my life

I need to be free of the dangers in my life

I need to be free of the children – kids that are causing me pain – grief.

It's not fair to me hence I need to be me. I need to live for me. I need to be truly happy.

Michelle Jean
December 08, 2013

In life you can only give so much before you collapse and burn out. And I've burnt out hence my many ailments in life right now.

You can only do so much before you drop down. And I'm at that stage because many times I have to hold on hence I faint, drop down.

Goodness pays but it does not pay when you put your enemies before you.

You have to put yourself first before you put others because at the end of the day, those that you help are truly not there for you. Hence a good friend is truly hard to find in this day and time. (Stephen Marley – False Friends)

We all want and when we get we do not remember others.

We do not think of others.

Never do to get and always remember the ones you are good and kind to are not always good and kind to you.

Michelle Jean
December 08, 2013

What mood should I be in Dear God because I so do not feel like myself.

I am so broken that I truly do not know what to do anymore.

I am truly fed up of the pain, the problems that face me hence I have to cry to you today even though I don't want to.

Trust me I am feeling it hence I truly want to run away. I need to run away. I need to find me because being a single parent sucks. Its way too hard but I have to bare the pain and suffering. I have to go through it because it seems sufferation is my way of life.

It seems sufferation is what you ordained for me.

How much more must I bare – face before you rescue me.

How much more pain must I feel before you see that I truly can't take anymore.

I am broken God, truly broken. Hence I cannot overstand nor comprehend why you would want to see your children suffer and in pain.

What have we done for you to abandon us like this? Yes I know the cleanliness rule but God –

Good God, but couldn't you truly look down upon me and infinitely and indefinitely stop my stress and problems – pain? All of them Good God including the stresses and pain concerning my children.

Good God mi no waane drop dung. You heard what my children's father said to me in regards to helping his son – my child – our child.

He told me he cannot help me because he can't deal with the stress.

Good God what stress? He doesn't even know how his children eat or if they need a pair of socks or shoes. But you know what, I am still holding on. He said his son is a big man and not a teenager.

Good God tell me what has he truly done for my boys.

This is his son – our son that needs help and you as a father cannot help him because he's twenty. Wow.

Tell me Good God what fatherly advice has he ever given my children – our children – his sons?

Wow.

Like I said, Genesis said women were to feel the pain of child birth and we are truly feeling the pain of raising our children because the fathers leave us alone to raise them by ourselves. This is our curse as women. We were to feel the pain because of men. Lying and deceitful men who care not for their children.

Lying and deceitful men that go from here to there deceiving women and children.

Lying and deceitful men that care not if their children are fed or even have a proper roof over their head (s).

Lying and deceitful men that have not a care in the world because all they have to do is move on to their next victim. Hence ole people sey oman bring dem troubles (belly) home and di man dem leave it (the belly) outside.

They were so right because it's us that feel the labour pain.

It's us that feel the pain raising our children alone.

It's us that cry out to you Good God for mercy and guidance – help raising our bad ass pickney dem.

You've seen my struggles from then to now and I am still struggling, hence I say you don't want to see me prosper.

You don't want me to be prosperous.

You don't want to see me amount to anything in life.

You don't want to see me happy and stress free.

You don't want to see me in a proper home – a clean home and environment.

I have to bare my earthly pains alone. Hence I will tell everyone that want and need a good and true mate to bug you for them.

Bug you Good God for good and clean children, obedient and honest children before they have any. It is imperative we do this in the living including ask you for life time partners that are not infidels. Lifetime partners that are good, clean and honest. (2) children is the norm but you can have 4, 5 or 6 even 7 if you can handle them, provide and feed them, care for them including give them the same or equal amount of true love.

Every child deserves a father and mother in their lives. Hence I cannot comprehend war.

I cannot comprehend why a next man would fight for what's not his.

I cannot comprehend why lands would send another man or woman's child to fight – kill.

I cannot comprehend the scope of this because according to the book of sin, one of your commandments Good God said, "thou shalt not kill," but yet we disobey you and disrespect your law anyway. We send men and women on the battlefield including children to fight – kill.

We do all that is wrong and expect to get right.

We use children in our nasty little games without thinking of their well being.

We say we love but have not truth – true love. Not even for our kids – children.

So tell me now Good God, how can you have true love for us when we can't even have truth – true love for our own?

Michelle Jean

Good God I will forever tell people – everyone to know their colours.

Know how you speak – talk to them because you do not speak all the time. Sometimes you take a break from everyone. I know this for a fact hence I do not see everything all the time. I see my life and the problems in my life and at times I cannot decipher my dreams – visions. Sometimes I can't remember what I see. This is life I guess until you have nothing else for me to do.

Like I said you see my struggles. You see and know the words of my first two's father.

You more than infinitely and indefinitely know the works of my last two's father hence I more than infinitely and indefinitely cling to you. Hence I know the wickedness of man in the living as well as in the spiritual realm. Wow do I ever know it. Man do I every know it hence I've felt the pain of both words and I will tell everyone to live good, clean and honest – true because the grass is definitely not greener on the other side. Trust me the other side is filled with pain, more pain than you feel on earth.

If you think you feel pain now just wait until tomorrow – the death of flesh.

Earthly pain is a walk in the park compared to spiritual pain and suffering.

Earthly pain is nothing compared to spiritual pain hence I tell you to live good, clean, honest and true.

Fear not the living or the dead if you are good but if you are evil truly woe be unto you.

You were told ***TRUTH IS EVERLASTING LIFE.*** This is true because Good God does not like liars nor does he like lies.

Lies and beauty is what took us out of his domain – kingdom and we can no longer afford to do this anymore. Like I've told you, certain people we are not to marry or be around not because of skin colour but because of lies. These people's god and gods are not ours. Hence they have no truth in them. They lie to humanity to bring all in humanity to hell and burn.

Like I've told you, evil is loyal to evil and if you are good then evil destroys you as well as set you up and even kill you. Hence death has hell but Good God has his kingdom of good and righteousness – truth.

Michelle Jean

Yes I feel the pain and I have to bare it hence at times I feel all alone.

I've done the work of you Good God now the ball is in your court literally. Now it's up to you to decide where you want to go from there.

I did go South hence that leg of my journey is fully done.

I did abide by you now it's up to you to make your people – children listen. It's up to you to now abide by us and let us including me be free.

It's up to you to help your people clean your land and lands up.

It's up to you to keep them safe now.

It's up to you to truly be with them.

I truly do not know if my journey ends now with you and if it does I truly thank you for the lessons learned and learnt. But 2014 is it between me and you because like I said, I would rather leave you with my dignity intact than to go to hell and burn for you or with you.

I fully comprehend you but the obedience part is hard and was hard because we don't always follow thru.
We've become so disobedient that we truly forgot how to listen.

I know life isn't always a cup of tea hence the yoyo effect in some of our lives as well as between me and you.

Yes like some of you, I have it hard. God – Good God said to write he never said he was going to make my life easy or even stress free.

He never said he was going to help me to make my children become clean.

He never said he was going to make my children listen to me.

He never said he was going to make them obedient.

He gave me the information – tools to give to you and I've done so. In all that I need to do, I have to do it and do it good – clean. Yes I cuss but I cannot change that. Yes I truly love my children hence soon I will escape them and the trouble they give. Trust me they had better pray and ask God – Good God for obedient, good, clean and honest children because the trouble they gave me, truly woe be unto them hence I truly, infinitely and indefinitely more than truly forgive them for all the stress – problems they've given me in the living.

Yes it's regrettable that I am walking away in 2014 but the pain.

I cannot go the journey alone because it does get lonely. And yes I know it's not Good God that is causing me pain. He's shown me what is to befall me but I am tired of the obeah working business by nasty and deceitful men and woman.

I just want and need a stress free life with Good God without the interference of sin and evil – wicked and sinful demons that cause me pain.

Hence Good God I am going to jump the gun here and say this to you. Our relationship is our relationship and yu chat mi business. No, I should not accuse you but I am going to anyway.

Yes mi chat yu but you did tell me to write and I am writing. The one thing I do not need from you is for you to bring an outsider into our relationship. These people or this person knows nothing about me nor do they know the relationship or of the relationship between me and you. I care not to associate myself with them. Like I've told you and have said, a dirty man or woman, pastor or clergy cannot make me clean, they can only make me dirty – unholy.

I come to you with my problems and troubles and I would like it to stay that way.

I know the evils of man and what they are doing to me hence I put you in the midst of my life.

I put you in all that I do as well as want and need you. So please keep the devil out of my domain because they are not wanted or appreciated – needed. This is our domain Good God hence you truly complete me in a good and true way.

You are all of me in a good and true way so please truly let us stay this way – good and true forever ever okay.

You've kept me so far and it's you alone that has brought me through the storm and storms, hence I am truthful – infinitely truthful to you in all that I do.

So truly keep the devil out. Nothing that he does can rock me because in all he tries to do I take my anger and pain to you as well as out on you. I will not change this hence I am harsh with you in virtually all that I do.

Michelle Jean

Life is not always easy and at times we get broken and want to give up.

We cannot see the light in the darkness because the pain is too great.

You want to give up because you feel there is nothing left for you to do. Many negative thoughts come. Trust me it's okay to want to give up. I want to, need to, but no matter how I tell myself I am giving up something in me keep me from giving up.

Giving up is not my weakness. It just means you have come to a cross road that's like an unbreakable brick wall that you cannot penetrate or go around or over.

You beat up on yourself and God – Good God because the avenues you've tried you've failed. All the doors are closed to you. You tell yourself you cannot face the troubles anymore.

Suicide comes into play for many including me
The tears and fears come
The pain and heartache
Doubt

Man you are plagued by financial stress
Health woes

You don't even know what to do or where to begin

Trust me I don't know what to do at times. I see things but yet I cannot pinpoint my life.

I do not know what God – Good God want or need for me. Meaning I do not know what he as in stored for me.

You're saying but you see things you can tell what's going to happen in the future.

True but in all I seek on earth and in the spiritual realm no one can help me. I've asked and tried but the ones I've asked can't help me so I am no different from you. Hence I've asked God – Good God why he does not want to see me prosperous.

Physical fight is nothing compared to spiritual fight because you are affected all around. If it is ordained in the spiritual realm that you will not move forward for 7 years or even 1 year, there is no way in hell that you will move forward. All that you try and do you will fail. Nothing anyone on earth try will help you because they cannot. Hence you do not go in the realm of the dead. You just bare your pain until you are released from this spiritual prison.

If a human being has gone to obeah man, witches or whatever medium they use to keep you down, then truly good luck in breaking this spell. You have to be strong because these people use the dead – demons to keep you down.

They use whatever means possible for you to lose it all including your life.

You know you are to be successful but they take your financial prosperity from you.

You know you are to have a good job but they take that from you.

You cannot live in peace hence they do all for you to lose the very home and apartment you live in.

They put you a way so that if you need help, no help is to come to you financially.

They make it so hard that you can't find a man or woman – that good someone.

If you are married and you are living good with your lifetime partner and or mate they do all for that person to leave you.

In so doing some walk with your name on parchment paper to keep you down.

Some give you certain pens to write with to keep you down.

Some give you certain food and drink to kill you literally.

All these things I know and more hence at times I see my mother and others. I know when the dead is around me because all that's around me, do not come to kill me but to protect me from the evils that are thrown at me. There is evil dead and there good dead. The good dead are your protectors. Hence I've told you I was told by the White Man in Blue to walk before death. He was of the spiritual realm hence I tell you about the color blue and how powerful it is.

I've also told you female death is a bitch because she does not care. And if you get her angry she will take you without a care.

It is not an easy road for me hence my battle is not just with humans but with spiritual evil as well. My mind and body is taking a beating but soon it will be over and woe – truly woe be unto these people for what they have done to me and others.

These people will do all to take it from you even kill you. This is how evil operates and this is what evil and wicked people do.

Some literally kill you hence I've told you about the lodge man society – the Abrahamic Order of the Dead. The Abrahamic Order is the highest order you can belong to because you are dealing directly with death himself hence human and animal sacrifices unto death – the dead. This order falls under the Order of Melchesidec – Satan himself.

Yes the churches belong to this order as well because they tell you to drink blood – literally accept death – die.

Like I've said, I know who is doing this to me hence I truly leave him to death – hell. Hell is every righteous and good person's victory over all that is evil. I worry not about evil doers hence I leave them alone. I infinitely and indefinitely know they are a part of the living dead hence they are the begotten of the dead. Revelations.

I've told you death knows me and female death is worse than male death. I know what female death looks like and trust me she hates my ass more than Satan does in my book. She wants me but she cannot have me. I do not fear her. I know how deadly she is hence I was told to walk before death and I've told you this already. Death is nothing new to me hence I truly put my trust in Good God and God. I have to because if I don't I would have been dead already. He's keeping me *hence I tell you about both worlds and hope you will comprehend and live.*

So on this if you are going through hardships and pain listen to these songs.

Tessanne Chin   **Anything's Possible**
Duane Stephenson   **Misty Morning**
Fred Hammond   **No Weapon**

Mr. Vegas   **Rise Again**
This song I dedicate to all that are in pain and going through the struggle. You can and will rise again just give it time.

Yes the prison walls cage you and surround you but you will make it. You can break those walls down and when you do, live truly for you and by your truth and honesty.

The devil will do all to hinder you and you will want to give up and do give up but after all is said and done rise up, dust yourself off and pray to Good God. Pray clean and true. He does help and it's okay for you to be angry at him and say he's no help to you. I've told you and will forever ever tell you never hide your true feelings from him. Be infinitely honest and truthful with him and to him. He is slow in help but he is sure.

Know that in all evil and his people have and has done to me I'm still standing.

I'm still breathing because I keep my hands and heart clean. Hence Good God is in the midst of all that I do that is good and true.

See I know the goodness of the ones he Good God has and have given me, hence I pray in my way to Good God.

I give him some of my goodness.

I give my dead mother some of my goodness.

I give my children and the seeds he Good God has and have given me some of my goodness because I am accountable for them.

See in the living if someone is good to you you can give them some of your goodness so that they can live. In so doing, when they pass on and they need one goodness that goodness that you gave to them in the living will go on their record – slate of good. This is why I bug Good God about my mother more times because I knew her goodness in the living hence I more than infinitely truly love her. Trust me nothing can happen to her in the grave hence I know she is secure with Good God and nothing that evil –

the devil do to me can take her and her goodness from me.

If you are good to your children in the living they can save you in death but it's not all that can or will save you. Hence not all sins are forgiven; hence the judgement of man – humanity in death – the grave.

Tamela Mann   *Take Me to the King*
I truly love this song because we go to God – Good God with our problems – troubles and it's as if he does not hear us.

We talk to him and it's as if our talk is in vain.

We become discouraged and tired.

We feel neglected and tired.

At times we become weak and without hope.

We become burdened down but you – we cannot give up. The spirit in you refuses to give up.

When we give up for a day our spirit tell us to try this avenue and that avenue.

Hence I say, do not give up on you nor give up on your passion – destiny. The doors that are closing are not the right doors. Yes evil hinders you but don't give up. One day Good God will move the devil out of your way the right way.

Yes you are rocked by don't give the enemy the victory over you.

Yes I can say don't give up because I want and need to give up but you cannot. My journey is not easy it is incredibly hard. I so don't like hard. I am the one to write 24 seven if I have to, but when it comes to advertising and pushing for these books to be known I so do not like it. But I have to do it because Good God called me alone and not me and someone else. Plus too the spiritual realm is infinitely not easy to deal with. So for me, don't give up joy cometh in the morning and remember the morning can be 3 – 9 months even years down the line.

Like I've told you I am no different from you. Books that I've written I cannot release. Man 2013. I've seen so much that I've put in book form and as 2013 closes I am hearing about deaths.

Hollywood deaths wow. I did see the deaths and the book that I've written that tells of the death I've not published but by the time this book is published it will be. Right now I'm just watching the visions unfold.

Hopefully I'll get to it (this book) and by then many things will be old news.

America I am watching – waiting because woo Nelly I so don't want to be any of you.

I don't want to be many Black People because many will be out of a job real soon.

Many will be enslaved again because many do not own a thing.

Time will tell because the time has come and 2014 and beyond will be a true testament and test of time for billions upon earth.

Below I told you of what I saw at the end of 2013 hence it's up to all of you.

Michelle Jean

God – Good God why is it that you keep letting the devil interfere in my life.

Why is it that you continuously allow evil – the devil to take my financial wealth – prosperity?

I need my prosperity – financial wealth and it's not right for you to allow others to take it from me.

I am tired of it because you do not want me to be prosperous financially, spiritually, health wise.

Tell me something now. What right do you have to continue to allow evil and wicked people to kill and hurt messengers?

What right do you have to let evil take away my prosperity?

What right do you have to keep me caged in prison?

No for real Good God, what right do you have to do this? I know I am over stepping my boundaries but you are failing us including me.

Babylon does not fail the devil.

Babylon has and have succeeded in slandering and killing your people and you are okay with this.

Tell me something. What right do you have to aid the devil and his children to defeat you?

What right do you have to aid the devil in killing – slaughtering your messengers?

The will of the devil will always be the will of the devil and that is evil.

True evil cannot change his or her evil ways hence the XX otherwise known as 4 – the square.

We know this to be 3XY. 3 females to 1 male. The daughters and father of sin – Satan. The mother belongs not to this and you know that. This has to do with the father and children of death.

Like I've said God, you cannot continue to aid sin – evil in their quest to dominate and control it all. You are wrong in doing so.

You cannot say I cannot go into a dirty domain and keep your children in filth. Come on now.

You cannot continue to let sin dirty the lives of humans. Like I said, you are allowing sin access to man – humanity and you cannot continue to do this. You want us to be clean but yet you continue to allow us to be manipulated and controlled by sin. Tell me this, how does that work from a cleanliness standpoint?

How does this work from a righteousness standpoint?

How does this work from a truth standpoint?

How does this work from a honest standpoint?

Sin is sin and it cannot be clean.

Tell me this now. If you continue to allow this to happen to man- humanity when it comes to sin and death, how can you say you as God and Good God is clean?

Death or sin has his book which he's deceiving many by so what say you?

You showed me how truthful a lie can be and seem because the lie came from a Russian White Jew. Hence I know the lie that was told to Eve (Evening) and you cannot under any circumstances let the lie continue. You too will be at fault Good God because you did not put a stoppage to it.

Billions are going to lose their lives because of this lie and you too are to blame Good God because you allowed it to happen.

You bargained away the lives of humanity for what?

Life isn't a game Good God it's real. We are not animals even though we act worse than them.

Like I said, your track record is not that good hence you need to do something and bring every wicked man and woman including children, spirit and beast to justice.

If you don't do this what is the point of humanity trusting you?

You want and need clean people but how can people be clean living in an unclean world – lands?

Sin has and have polluted it all but you don't seem to care. Well you have to care because not one of us said we wanted to be born in an unclean environment or a dirty planet to dirty and unclean people. Come on now.

Don't even go there with the choice because on this day it does not wash with me.

You have a right and an obligation to your people because I saw this message written on the school wall and it said, "for God so love us he is worthy to be praised." Hence I teach it because that was your intent.

Now I say unto you. Under no circumstances can you say you love us so and let sin and evil, wicked and evil human beings continue to hurt your messengers, children and people. By letting this happen you are telling me literally that you lied. You are a liar and cannot be trusted. You are also telling me you truly hate us because you continue to aid the devil in killing your people plain and straight.

So you truly need to look into yourself Good God for the truth – the true truth.

You cannot say you love us so and watch our prosperity be taken away from us.

You cannot say you love us so and watch your children go hungry – unfed.

You cannot say you love us so and watch evil and wicked people destroy Africa and Jamaica just like that including me.

You cannot say you love us so and watch your people become homeless and enslaved once again.

None of this is true love it's hatred. True hatred because like I said, you are aiding evil to condemn and kill your people – children. Life is not a game nor a sport and if it is a game to you then you should not be God or Good God, you should be called Evil – True Evil – the Devil.

No I am not losing respect I am just telling you like it is.

You forbid me to go into my homeland which you deemed dirty – unclean but yet you permit others to go into a dirty land – country. Now tell me how fair and just are you?

You forbid me to go into my homeland which you deemed dirty - unclean but yet you keep us in unclean lands.

You forbid me to go into my homeland which you deemed as dirty – unclean but yet you permit dirty and evil people to harm me – take all from me.

Tell me, how is that loving us so or even loving me so?

Is that not hatred on your part?

Is that not evil on your part?

And no, I cannot speak on the behalf of others but you are infinitely and indefinitely wrong because people do not know that you have and has deemed Jamaica unclean. All I've done to let people know this I've failed. So tell me now, who is the unjust and unfair one?

Who hates me?

Like I said, you are aiding the devil and hindering me from doing your good work.

You cannot do this anymore because like I said, sin is loyal to death and it's not right for people to go to hell unnecessarily.

Many things can be avoided but you give evil the victory over humanity instead of truly helping your children – good children and people to do your good and true work.

The spell of sin must be lifted hence you need to truly be in the midst of all that I do that is good and true.

You need to be with your people as well as be in the midst of them.

Yes death must take his people and maybe that's why you don't want me to succeed in telling the world that Jamaica is unclean. But Good God people need to know the truth.

You cannot deem a land unclean and let good and evil go into that land that is wrong. Like I said, I would infinitely never ever run into a burning building to save my enemy. My duty is to call the police and or fire department and report the fire. My enemies are my enemies and I am infinitely not responsible for them nor would I take responsibility for them, but they too have to know. You know what let me stop because it seems I am defending evil and I cannot do that. What you deem as right I cannot say is wrong because I am infinitely not you nor can I be you.

Evil must go but you have to tell evil that and you've been doing this because I write about evil in these books.

You cannot spare evil but like I said. They must know their end and that is what you've been doing.

Just do me a favour. Do not let your good and true people go into Jamaica. Do that much for them because I know the collapse of evil's system at the end of 2013. I do not know which land or lands will collapse financially hence I will leave the devil alone. His time has come to collapse and I truly hope you infinitely and indefinitely never ever let any of the devil's land and kingdom rise again. They must never rise again because of the evil and wickedness they have done to man, earth, you, the trees, water, animals and spirits of the land. They took all from us and for this they must truly pay literally.

Michelle Jean

Tell me something Good God, the wages of sin is death but yet sin keeps on sinning.

Now tell me this, why can't sin infinitely and indefinitely die?

Do you love sin more that man – humanity?

No for real Good God. Do you love, truly love sin more than man – humanity?

The law states the wages of sin is death and truth is life everlasting but yet sin cannot die.

Please do not give me the 24000 years that was allotted to sin because what's good for the goose is definitely good for the gander. So since sin had 24000 years to deceive and kill, I am asking you to give good, all that is good and true, infinite and indefinite forever ever goodness on earth. Good hath no time to die because goodness and truth is life everlasting, it cannot die. So as of 2014 let the harvest take sins children – the children of death – wicked and evil people including spirits and beast. They can never ever come back to earth. The domain and kingdom of earth must be true, good and clean now. Let truth, cleanliness, goodness and honesty reign supreme forever ever on earth with you. Also, let your goodness be in the midst of all we do forever ever.

Sin can't have it all. Come on now.

Sin cannot get away with sin any longer. Come on now.

And please do not use sin is not my child with me because it does not wash. Sin is hindering me and you are allowing it to happen.

Your children should not have to cry for you or to you constantly for help.

I've told you, I do not want or need to be a part of sins kingdom but you constantly ignore me.

Tell me something. Is it just for sin and evil to take away my prosperity of wealth and leave me penniless all the time?

Is it right for me to be left in the streets without anything?

Is it right for evil to hinder me every step of the way?

Now tell me this. How can you say you love us so or even love me so and let all these things happen to us including me in the living and in the spiritual world – realm?

When this happens will your children not look to you as a true failure because you saw our needs and failed to help us?

You allowed us to be whipped brutally.
You allowed us to be chained like dogs even classed and called dogs.

Beggars

You allowed the hatred of us to happen.

You allowed us to be killed at the hands of rapists and murderers.

You allowed sins evil and wicked children to rule, dominate and control us.

You allowed sin's evil and wicked children to cause us to go against you with their lies and brutal beatings – deceit.

You allowed our history – beautiful history and heritage to be defiled and distorted by sin's wicked and evil children – race.

You allowed the poisoning of our children and people. So what say you about loving us so and letting crap – sins of brutality like these to happen to your children – people?

Now tell me how can you love us so, when all you have for us is pure hatred just like sin and death – the so called devil who is you on this day in my book.

And yes I know you are not the devil but to what is happening to us you are in my book on this day.

Evil need to be stopped infinitely and indefinitely and if you can't stop him then who will?

Who will stop the devil and his race?

Who will shut sin and death down infinitely and indefinitely – permanently? Come on now.

If you do not have the power and strength to stop all facets of sin and evil – the devil, then who has?

Are we lost and without hope under your reign?

I have to ask you these questions Good God because something is not right somewhere and I cannot pinpoint the error, hence my doubt of you. I am truly sorry but I have to bring doubt into this on this day.

Michelle Jean

Yes God – Good God you can get upset at me but I have to tell you like it is and right now to the way I feel, I truly have nothing to lose.

If you want someone fake to defend you as well as speak to you then by all means go right ahead and find someone else. Release me from our decree. I will be on my way but it will be your loss and my good gain because I would be free to be me.

Like I said, you cannot say you love us so and watch sin including sinful and wicked people – evil people that reside in sinful land and lands destroy your people including you and your dignity.

Loving us so should not mean hatred on your part.

Like I said, what belongs to the devil stays with the devil. It's his, leave him the hell alone. Don't bleeping want what's his because he's not clean, he's dirty.

Secure your people – children – your good people that are with you. Right now I am so tired of talking to you because you're as stubborn as a mule and as stubborn as me in some ways. And don't even think it or go there because you are.

Stick no pap inna yu ease ole.

Yahno mule

Yahno pickney so grow the hell up and do better. And don't even dare look at me and my life. Don't go there lest I blast you again.

Loving us so is not hurting us.

Loving us so is not aiding the devil to destroy us.

Loving us so is not aiding the devil to kill us.

Loving us so is not aiding the devil to take away our heritage, wealth, good health, truth of you.

Come on now.

You can't want us to praise you and you're not helping us to get rid of all that is sinful. Come on now.

The devil loves but good life, clean life; honest life is truth – eternal and forever ever good and clean. Come on now.

Do not use me or lie to me because I will walk away from you just like that and you know this. Come on now.

I am not being rude I am telling you what I will do if you do not stop with the lies. I am tired of you aiding death.

I am tired of you lying. If you truly love us then truly love us. Do not give us basket with holes to carry water.

When you do this, how can we trust you in anything that you do?

Like I said, below I saw the White Man in gray and he emptied the hour glass and this had to do with an economic collapse at the end of 2013.

Yes I think the sand came back up right away. *But let the rising of the sand of time quickly be that of Good and not of evil come on now. Let good rise quickly and keep this financial goodness and prosperity forever ever. Also if this financial prosperity pertains to me let me keep this good financial prosperity forever ever so that I can help your good and true people, lands as well as you and earth.* You have to be infinitely and indefinitely be in the midst of my goodness and our goodness all the time. This is my true and good request of you because despite my harsh ways with you, you are more than infinitely truly loved by me.

Michelle Jean

It's December 22, 2013 and I can't make anything of these dreams. Maybe you can help because I will not try to decipher anything because I've been on the war path with God in regards to sin and what is happening in the world.

This dream I could not remember but after listening to music I remembered part of it.

I was lying down in my bed and I saw this hourglass. The hourglass was almost empty and this White Man in a grey suit did something and the sand in the hourglass quickly came down to naught at the end of 2013. I said no because I was scared. The hourglass or sand in the hourglass represented the economy and thought the economy was going to collapse. Suffice it to say I did not see the economy crash. I cannot remember the rest of the dream but I think after the sand went down at the end of 2013, the hourglass quickly filled up again with sand. I am pretty sure it filled up again. So if someone know how to decipher this dream then go ahead and let me know.

I also dreamt I went into my bathroom and a tall box of Sunlight Detergent in the yellow box was beside my toilet. The box was on the right side of my toilet and it was unopened. The box was not fat but skinny and high. Not higher than the toilet if you are interested to know. I so do not know what these dream represent or mean. So if you can shed some light on them like I said, please let me know because like I said, I was arguing with God.

See 2013 has shaped up to be a disastrous year for me because December 19th my last child confronted his bully that was talking smack about his family and he was sent home.

My ex husband presented me with court papers to go to court January 27th of 2014 for child support.

Now people this man does not know how my two boys eat and drink.

He's never bought them a Christmas present or called them to wish them happy birthday and he's taking me to court to pay him back child support of $5741.00. His children with me are over 18 years old and according to him they are not going to school.

People I will not get upset because like I told my sister, if I had the money to pay him back all the child support he's ever paid me, I would. He pays $240.00 for two boys and they are in school. My first son is in his final year of college and moving on to university to get his degree and the second one you know about him if you have read my other books. Well you know about him because you've read the top part of this book.

I've had to stand up firm for him to get his high school diploma. He got it in June of 2013. Now the task is to get him to go on to college.

That would be a milestone for me if he could get into college for September 2014. Trust me if I could light up the universe with elation, I would because I so want and need him to go on to college.

Oh man I've let you into my personal life again. But hey we are a family – true family right? Well I hope so because like I said, I am no different from you.

Family you know me by now. I am not a fighter hence you know the trials and tribulations I go through with my children.

This man have never bought my children a candy for their birthdays and Christmas. Good God can stand up and speak – tell you that I do not bother this man. I left him alone over the years to raise my children by myself. I am one to say fuck you if you don't want to be a father to your children. I refuse to run you down to be a father to my children. You are a man you should know you have children. I don't call him for anything. A part from calling him and asking him for money to buy graduation clothes for his second child because I truly could not afford it after how many years of not calling him.

My son went to his prom but he did not graduate because he was missing credits. He finally got all his credits this year and trust me I am proud of him. I also truly, infinitely truly thank God – Good God because my son said he heard a voice say school or something pertaining to that but I can't remember the exact words he told me today. He tried his best to get into school and he got accepted at a different high school from his home school. Yes when he needed help he came to me and I helped him.

I also called him on another occasion and asked him for some money to buy groceries for his children and he said he could not help me. Hence I have to say thank God for my sister and brothers because they helped me in my time of need.

Family, I do not bug this man and this is over 10 years of not seeing this man and not asking him for anything I am asking him for help. I've raised our children on my own and he cannot say I've bugged him in anyway.

The financial burden has always been on me even when I got sick I did not bug him. I ended up in the hospital for almost two weeks. My oldest son missed his prom because he was at home taking care of his siblings while I was in the hospital.

Like I said, I am not going to run behind a man and say come and take your child or take care of your child. You are a man, you should know to take care of your children hence he's never exercised his rights as a father.

Listen my children have been through enough.

Read Bodaciously You from my other line of books because the young years of my first child in that book is the young years of my son when it came to disappointment.

My first son broke his leg at a young age and we called him and told him his son broke his leg and was in the hospital. Until this day he has not shown up.

I remember the days when I would drop our first son at school and by the time I got to work the school would call me and tell me to come get my son because he was in pain. No I did not call him because I know he would not come and yes

I found out what ails my son and he does not know until this day.

I don't bug this man and the week before Christmas you are giving me court papers to go to court because you don't want to pay child support anymore and you want back pay.

Family, money is something I will infinitely and indefinitely never ever forever ever never ever fight a man or anyone for or over.

Fuck you if you think I am going to fight you for your money. I would rather tell you what parts of your mother you can go and find with your money.

No. I am different when it comes to money hence I truly thank God – Good God for my upbringing. My grandmother instilled values in us. My mother did the same. I remember my grandmother telling us don't be red eyed for people's things and I refuse to be red eyed for anyone's things. I would rather walk naked in the fucking street and even when I am naked and destitute in the streets. And all when I am naked and destitute in the streets, I refuse to be red eyed for your things or fight with you over money or your responsibilities in life.

Fuck him – fuck him until he can't fuck himself anymore. Hence I regret the day that my sister told me to take his ass to court. I hate courts hence I should have stayed out but I know she was looking out for the best interest of my children.

I was not charging him for child support because we came to the agreement for him to pay $300.00 per month for our children and he agreed. Suffice it to say he did not pay and that is when my sister said to take his ass to court and so it stand until this day. *I left him the hell alone.* And no he did not pay his child support regularly; he's always been in arrears, now to have this. But I should of known he was never a man or father because he did not support his two boys in Jamaica.

Trust me I want nothing to do with this man and am I bitter. Yes I am bitter that he was not there for his children.

I am bitter that he did not contact me and ask me to issue a stop order on child support payments. He would have known that I did not renew the payment allowance.

In Canada if the government is helping you in anyway, any child support payments go to them.

Hence I have to get my health in check because I hate being sick.

Yes my health is improving slowly but like I said, if I could give him back every penny I got in child support, I would not hesitate to do so because he was never and will never be a father to my children.

Who the fuck is he anyway? I never stopped him from seeing his children because he had and still has legal rights to see them. If he wanted to see his children and since I am hindering him from seeing them, why the hell did he not take me to court and say judge, my ex wife does not want me to see my children. I went to her house on these dates and she denied me access to them.

Why the hell did he not show up at my door with the police and say I will not allow him to see his children and I want to see them because I have a right to them every other weekend. Or even tell the judge – take my ass to court like I said and tell the judge that he wants me to drop our children off at the police station or a safe house on his turn to see the children.

Every child deserves a father and I am not like those fuckry mothers that use their children in their nasty little scunt ass fuckry games. I fucked with you and got them. Therefore, when you and I are not together, I should not use them as a fucking pawn in any jealous rage or any money games. ***Fuck all of that because life is not a fucking game of what I can get from what I cannot get out of a fucking man. Dicks are free and some can be bought. You just have to lay yourself careless for one to be stuck inside of you by a man and I refuse to lay myself careless hence I am without a man and without a plastic dick.***

This is me. Take me as I am so fuck him. I ***am a fucking proud black woman that is more than proud of the way my grandmother and mother raised me. I never saw none fought a dick or a man for what they have.***

And for all of you that are asking. I did not hit him up for alimony payments. When I fucking hate and despise a man I want nothing from you; not even the use of your fucking name. I don't want your fucking money to support me because we are fucking done. Am a different woman hence I am the way I am. Yes I have to change my health and bank card all others have been changed.

Come to me as a man. I don't fucking bite. I may look like a fucking pit bull but that's it. I have my values that I live by don't clown me or do that to me. But like I said, some men are not men, they are less than dogs. Yes he did call me to say he had something important to talk to me about and I was telling my first son that I think he wants to talk to me about his child support. I had the feeling it was about this but I was not expecting to get court papers the week before Christmas. Wow.

I don't fucking bother you don't fucking bother me. Talk to me. I am not about money when it comes to bitches. I bug God – Good God for his money because his money is the only money that I want and need and he cannot say otherwise.

So to you my ex husband. Royally fuck you mother fucker because I have broughtupsy. My more than gorgeous and beautiful mother and grandmother raise me right mother fucker. Look at your stinking cesspool of an armhouse life and go fuck yourself. Burn in hell mother fucker because my children turned out right despite the trouble some of them give.

None a mi pickney dem no call yu an bug yu an beg yu fi anything.

Your money, $240.00 that they bumped up to $300.00 dollars just recently does not benefit my children because we don't get it. It goes to the government, it's them you owe and not me so truly fuck off.

Let me tell you something, my children meet it in life yes. And all when dem shoe bottom a tear out and slushy water from the snow freeze dem foot dem neva sey Mama call daddy an beg him a shoe fi mi.

Si dem dey, dem a baane hustler and worker because my first son work for all he's got and him tek telling. All when people rob him of his $1700.00 for his first car he listened to me. Mi tell him, let it go and him listen. And I know Good God highly favours him and has blessed him because soon he will be done college.

My second child, it's his friends and the bad company that I don't like because him a baane hustler. When mi sick and in need of food in the house him hustle with his electronic and help me put food on the table. Like I said, it's his friends that I complain about because to me dem no right not all but some.

Nastiness no pass some because dem noa sey mi no like a nasty house and yes at times I am miserable. I know the kids I have because a dem mi si when mi sick. A dem cook fi mi and like I've said, my first son is my backbone because he takes telling and knows what to do if I am sick.

Money is something I infinitely and indefinitely trust all my children with and Good God knows this. My life that's different but it's getting better hence Good God is hearing me.

Damn wrenk

Dutty an stink

Bitch go check yourself because you're a fucking wreck.

Damn stink. Yu no si sey mi life blighted because of you.

Yu a carry dung. Damn obeah working rectobate. Yu live a obeah man because obeah man a yu god. A him a nyam yu money. ***But let me tell you this, no matter what yu obeah man do him caane rock my truth and true love when it comes to Good God because he's my keep. No matter the blows he throws to kill me as well as rob me for my wealth, health and prosperity, death cannot take me because I am not death's child nor am I one of his and her own.***

No matter how much he takes away my financial prosperity he cannot rock me because I am determined not to end up in the streets naked with my children. So all that your obeah man dem du, I truly leave them to Good God because on this day, December 24, 2013 in the name of God and Good God I truly curse them as well as truly curse every obeah man globally infinitely and indefinitely. I curse the day that they were born and banish them all to hell for infinite and indefinite lifetimes and generations. You do not hurt people. What they do, they willingly do for money. They willingly use evil to hurt another human beings and that is not right so curse be unto all of them from the day they were conceived and born onwards. None, absolutely none of their names can or will be written in the Good God's book of life. They are dead, hence they must go down with the dead to see the dead in hell. Praise be unto God – Good God because thy will be done. Amen

I refuse to tolerate shit now. I am not hurting you nor am I interfering with you or in your life, leave me the hell alone. I do not walk with sin or in sin hence I leave sin's children alone. I've been through too much at the hands of evil and wicked people in my lifetime to give sin and evil the victory over me.

Family you know my battle with death.

You know the blows that have come my way at the hands of death – the dead as well as with wicked and evil people. I've told you about the two white gentlemen in blue. Hence I know the power of the colour blue. One told me to walk before death and I've been walking before death. But when death – evil and wicked people disturb me I have to put a stoppage to it. I am not dead, I am alive hence I walk and talk with Good God in life – good life.

Like I said, I curse the day I met him and laid – slept with him. I do not regret my children even though when they stress me out I say I regret having them. But in true truth, I do not regret them hence I truly and infinitely bless my children with goodness and truth because they are mine. All that is good and true I bless them with because I felt the pain of raising them. Hence I truly dedicate them in goodness and in truth to the goodness and truth of good life and that good life is Good God himself and herself because he's both male and female. I truly bless their lives with goodness and truth and it's my hope that he Good God will continue to protect them as well as lift them up in goodness and in truth so that they too may walk forever ever in goodness and in truth with him. Not just them but their children and future generations. This I also ask of the good seeds and people he will now give me.

Ex husband yu no si Good God a keep an a bless me. I give God – Good God the glory despite what I've been through in life, because I know he too has met it in life with us humans.

Yes mi get down pan him because like I've said, he's my only friend and I refuse to change it. Yes my life gets boring but the one thing I have and can depend on to get me through is my music, my writing and children including some members of my family. I may be down but trust me I am certainly not out.

So fuck you bitch because I am more than highly favoured and blessed by my more than Precious King and Good God.

Coo pan yu to. A Mama alone raise fi mi pickney dem with the aid of God. Yes I tell him he's not there for me but he is despite my storms.

A him a keep mi all when mi want to end it when stress and pressure tek mi.

Remember you can't help yu pickney dem so don't you dare fucking lie pan mi bout mi a keep yu from yu pickney dem.

Yu rate or count dem? Bwoy fuck off because none a dem naa beg you nothing. Dem no count yu as a father.

None a dem a cum a yu ouse an a bug yu fi anything? I did not put it this way you did, so truly go chuck yourself and blow. Fuck you, Satan riffle and or saxophone a wait pan yu inna hell fi blow pan.

Cho nu get mi mad now because if mi get off hell cry literally.

Bwoy one piece of advice from mi. Walk good yu hear because hell no fucking pretty. An fi yu hell no pretty because a no mi abandon fi mi pickney dem a yu. Hence your spot in hell literally mother fucker. So truly walk and life you demon duppy.

Coo pan yu to. Sin betta looking dan yu to rass. Yu no si di sin wey dey pan yu. Wey yu no go clean yourself up if you truly can. Obeah a nyam yu out because yu wuk obeah and use obeah like bath water. Yu bayed inna obeah hence you are like unto the walking dead. Not even drangcrow want you. Hence leave me the fuck alone an no lie pan mi.

Remember a who pick yu up from nowhere and bring you somewhere. So truly check yourself because like I said, you're a fucking wreck.

Pickney caane raise dem self. Dem need two parents to raise them but I did it on my own with Good God standing by my side. Hence I did not do it alone.

All when mi give up him tell mi sey he's with me.

When mi feel mi enemy dem a rise up mi get No Weapons.

When mi truly give up mi get Anything's Possible.

I've gotten Rise Again – good music by different artist of all genre to help me heal hence many of these songs are in the Michelle Jean line of books.

I worry not about you because Good God has my back at all times.

To you my ex husband I curse the day I met you as well as curse the day I laid with you. You're a fucking curse.

As for you children that see your mother holding down the fort by herself, I keep telling you to stop giving trouble because it's not easy on her.

She is the important parent that is doing it for you.

Help her when she needs help. Like I said, I know my children and they do give trouble. I see certain things and I tell them but my second child refuse to listen to good council, hence I cannot trust him with my life when it comes to some of his friends.

My spirit cannot take them and I've told them that I don't like them because they do not heed good council.

It's good to want better for them but they have to want better for self. Some of them are from working class families with good jobs and it's them that are messing up their lives including my son messing up his.

I am not a saint because I gave my mother my share of troubles when it came to one particular friend and I am reaping the seeds of my sorrows sown when I was younger. Hence I tell you if you think it's peace and safety now, wait until tomorrow – when you have children of your own. Even if you don't want children and have none remember I told you this. You will feel it in old age because you don't know who will come and abuse you financially, sexually or whatever means of abuse people use.

If you have good parents or a good parent teaching you right and helping you, cherish them and do good because goodness grow up to Good God.

I don't bother with my enemies but when my enemies come into my way, I will get stinker than sin himself literally.

Leave me fuck alone if I've left you alone.

My children are mine and trust me I truly love them. I will defend them in goodness but I will not defend them when they are wrong. I will not condone their wrongs and they know this and will tell you this.

I truly love being around my children at times hence they can tell you I bug them to the point where they tell me Mama you need a man. They tell me I need to go out there and make friends and I would tell them I have a friend and that's God.

Yes my life is boring and I need a vacation, hence I bug God – Good God for one because I do need to get away from my kids. An all when mi dey pan vacation dem a get phone call every day. My children are my world in many ways hence I listen to them. I have a relationship with my children. When they do something wrong the school don't have to call me because I know, they tell me. The confrontation between my last child and this boy I knew would happen because my son did tell me he was going to confront this child. He does not like him talking smack about his family. I've been trying to quell him and hoping he would let it go but he could not.

Hence I've told some of you mothers that if unnu a raise hog fi keep dem inna dem pen and no let dem out in society.

It is not right for any child to be bullied. Some children do not take kindly to your children speaking smack about their families. It will and does get serious.

Guns and knives come into play and when your child gets hurt you hear that child had no right.

I will never advocate violence but it does happen and your child is to blame. You are not at school to know. Some of your children do bully kids and some can't take it hence some commit suicide. Now I am telling you this. ***Because of your child's actions you are held***

accountable for their actions in Good God's court of law. You will go to hell and burn next to your child because you did not council your child right. And yes I know some of you try but there is so much you can do as a parent if they do not want to listen to you. For this trying you are not held accountable. I am talking about the parents that know their bad ass kids are causing trouble and not do anything about it.

I know the bad asses I have because I teach my children to not lie to me or anyone. It don't always work hence they eventually get caught.

I do. Trust me when I do wrong I get caught right away. Good God don't make it slide trust me.

Like I've said, I am not a saint. I am just like you but certain things in my life I refuse to do hence my children know, if they father a child or children they had better be there for them. Trust me if dem no support dem pickney dem, a hell an powda ouse fi dem because all when mi dead dem naa go have a life. Truss mi every wey dem go dem wi si fi mi angry face and di fiya wey dem si dem betta smarten up.

No child asked to come into this world, we fucked and get them hence they are our responsibility. We are to raise them right and teach them right.

Yes for some of you it's hard but you can make that difference in your life.

Daddy is not there but you have Mama.

Some of you don't have Mama you have a father or a grandmother. They are still the important person in your life hence you have to help them in a good way.

As parents we don't have it easy either. Remember we have to work, cook, clean, do laundry, help you with homework hence the stress is great. So the little you do to help around the house is a great help.

If you know your job is to take out the garbage take it out.

If your job is to do the dishes do the dishes and if you can do your own laundry do it and don't wait for Mama to tell you to.

If you can make the salad for mommy or daddy or granny do it. That is something she does not have to do.

Clean up after you. The less talking she does the better it is for her and the less stress on her.

Mama sey go to school go to school. And to let you in on a little secret, Good God truly loves intelligence. He truly loves when you can read and write because his teachings are also in writings.

Never let anyone take away your goodness because when you lose it you will pay.

Yes some parents are miserable. Trust me I am and at times I truly want to leave my kids and make them feel it without me.

Trust me I would not have to fight with them for washing dishes, taking out the garbage, doing their own laundry and even waking them up for school.

Sometimes we say no go deyso. No go deyso. Jamaican parents are weird. Some of us go by our spirit and sometimes we say our spirit is not right. We can't explain it hence some of you that have Jamaican parents think us weird and foolish, but a no fool fool wi fool fool. It's the spirit in some of us.

I know not all parents are good hence never give up on doing good. ***Your parent's hell does not have to be your hell.***

Listen, evil is all around and evil destroys. So if you have a good parent do not destroy him or her because you need them.

You need to hold your head up because hell is real and you truly don't want to go there. You may not see what your parents are talking about now but when you have children of your own you will see and know.

Hold on to your good teachings and know that true love cannot hurt. A parent that loves you true only want and need what's best for you.

Yes I beat up on God – Good God and you can too because each and every day I am learning something. Evil does not like good and evil will do everything in its power to destroy and kill all that is good. This is why good people die young.

Good is a threat to evil hence evil has his book of sin that tell his people how to sin and kill.

I beat up on God – Good God because this is not right.

This morning December 22, 2013, I was beating up on him because I said he too is at fault for keeping the lie going and he's no different from the devil.

He cannot say he love us so and let evil kill and ridicule his people. That's not love or even true love it's hatred. He hates his people because he sits idly by and let evil and wicked people kill his people and spread hatred of them without remorse and that is not right.

I reminded him of Job and said he's a liar. He is clean, infinitely and indefinitely clean, so how can he talk to Satan.

In Job it said, "And God said to Satan have you considered my son Job?" Please do not quote me verse for verse or word for word because I do not have the book of sin or bible before me.

The book of sin further goes on to say, "God said to Satan do all that you will unto Job but do not take his life."

I know I've talked about Job before but not in depth. Now I told God he's a liar because he's clean and he's talking to Satan who is unclean.

I told him he hated Job's ass because he told Satan to do all to him but spare his life.

Now, if he truly loved Job he would not have told Satan to cause Job stress, pain and heartache hence he's no different from Satan – the devil himself. He caused Job pain.

He caused Job to lose his children and that was not right. He God caused Satan to take the life of Job's children hence he God – Good God is no different from death. He Good God is on the same level as death hence he Good God works with death. Family and people, I was so disgruntled. I was also thinking about Nelson Mandela and the 27 years he spent in jail for wanting goodness for his people.

I thought about Bob Marley and how they killed him before time.

I was thinking about Martin Luther King Jr. and how they assassinated him – murdered him.

I also went back into my Islamic history and said I wanted to send Blind Obsession Rebuttal – the Truth is Now or Never to Dr. York and found out via the internet that he was locked up in 2004 for child molestation.

When I read that I felt that pain to my stomach. Yes I know he's a fraud but child molestation is beyond my scope of reasoning hence I went to God and say. Despite the what his children do and this man was not a child of Good God, the devil find a way to shut you down.

They find a way to use children against you.

They find a way to use your own people against you.

They find a way to destroy you because they do not want Black People to be free or know the truth. They want us to forever be ignorant hence keeping us in hell with them.

Nothing that the devil do or does can be justified hence his people own the global market, governments and law societies including schools.

Trust me I quarreled with God brutal this morning and tell him he's not just because it's not right for the Black Race to endure and go through this.

What right does anyone have to want to destroy all blacks because of the colour of their skin?

What right does anyone have to keep the next man down because you fear them and the number 13?

No come on now. Life isn't about death it's about good life and everyone has a right to live. If you don't like a race of people ban them then from coming into your country. Don't have anything to do with them and in so doing stay the fuck out of Africa and all Black Lands. Come on now.

Like I said, I don't want your stinking worse than cesspool god and gods because dem stink worse than sin – shit so keep your demon duppies that you call gods to yourself. Don't fucking come into my land and or homeland and sell us your shit because we don't come into your home and or homeland and sell you our gods.

Your stink hole and stinking gods are not mine because I don't believe in death. I truly know life already and that life is Good God.

I don't want your dead gods to bring me to hell. I have Good God and all I have to do is live clean so when my spirit sheds its prison which is the flesh, I go up to Good God and not down to hell.

Don't try and control me because I will not be controlled by you or Good God himself. I don't business with you so stay away from me.

The devil's own is the devil's own and Good God is not concerned about the devil's people, he is concerned about his own. Hence we as messengers of God – Good God cannot go into the churches and shrines or temples, mosques and synagogue of the dead and interfere with the devil's children.

What belongs to the devil belongs to the devil and God – Good God will infinitely never ever interfere with them, hence billions are marked for death. Their names are in the book of the dead and not in the book of life.

These things I know hence I refuse to go to church and have since begged God – Good God forgiveness and pardon for once going into the domain of the devil.

I also got down on him for providing food and water for the devil's children.

I told him he's condoning slackness and aiding death to keep evil alive. I told him he should not be providing food and water for them because the devil's children is not his children. They belong to the devil hence the devil should feed them – his children.

What he's doing – proving food and water for the devil's own is wrong and he's doing wrong hence he too is a sinner – have sinned. So he too must infinitely and indefinitely go to hell and die.

You cannot say you are true love or love us so and watch us die. Watch death take innocent lives senselessly.

Family I'm sorry but I had to do it. I had to tell Good God like it is because what I see and know about him is not right.

You cannot truly love then turn around and aid death to massacre and kill your own children. Like I told him, Nelson Mandela did not have to go through this but he did anyway. He aided evil's children to lock this man up unjustly. No I am not Good God but just is just and right is right and he was wrong.

You cannot say you truly love your children – people and aid evil's children to hurt them like this. Come on now.

My ancestors went through slavery.

I've felt the pain at the hands of wicked and evil people and although I am still going, it did not have to be that way.

Evil should not kill and get away with it scot free. All you're telling me is that you don't give a fuck what evil and wicked people do to others.

Evil designed laws for his wicked and evil children and he Good God's children are caught in the cross fire and he God – Good God has done fuck all to take us – his people out of the cross fire of death.

Who the hell wants to suffer here on earth in the flesh only to go to hell and suffer even more and yes worse in hell? Come on now.

Like I said, I truly love Good God but there are days like these that I go off on him and voice my concerns.

Why should anyone suffer?

He's truth and he Good God does not block anyone from his kingdom, so why is he allowing wicked and evil – sinful people from blocking others from getting into his good and true kingdom – domain? Come on now.

How fair is that?

No I don't regret truly loving him Good God but he has to do a hell of a lot better when it comes to the justice of his people.

Stop letting evil hinder his people including me come on now.

Yes I am harsh hence the relationship Good God and I have I do not want or need it to change. He's my complete life even on the days when I get wrenk an stink and want to leave him infinitely and indefinitely.

Family, Good God is good life and it is only when we start living right and doing right that we will truly see him and comprehend him fully. Like I said, the devil is wrong and what the devil is doing to many is not right and he cannot idly sit by and watch it happen.

It's not fair nor is it right for evil to have a upper hand on good.

It's not fair for evil to kill and destroy.

It's not fair for anyone to go to hell and die. The lies of evil worked and it's time now for it to stop. It's time for Good God to speak and open his mouth and say no more.

Evil had 24000 years to do wrong because in truth every human being on the face of the planet is like Job. God – Good God did not talk to Satan it was Satan telling his people how to kill and massacre the children and people of Good God. He Good God would not be so vile and wicked as Satan because I've told you time and time again, Good God does

not deal in death death does. Sin deals in death because THE WAGES OF SIN IS DEATH but TRUTH IS LIFE EVERLASTING.

Hence if you are not living a truthful and clean life, a good life, you cannot have everlasting life.

There are no ands ifs or buts about this.

God – Good God is good all the time and no one should come and write books of lies about him.

It's time for it to stop because like I've said, sin violated the law of sin and for that he must die alongside his people right away.

The goodness of earth evil must not partake of. Evil must partake of evil which is the fire of hell hence it is them to go to hell right now. Right away. Good should not have to live in fear nor should good have to live amongst the unclean and unjust.

When he Good God continue to let this happen he too must be charged for sin and hindrance because he is hindering his people from becoming clean as well as living clean.

Yes this is the way I am with him on the days when something is not right with me or my spirit. Lies cannot prevail over the truth and if lies prevail over the truth then he Good God is not true. He will be and would be a liar just like sin and all evil – Satan himself.

Michelle

It's the day before Christmas – December 24, 2013 and Good God I hold my head and hands up to your glory and give you praise and thanks for keeping me and my children thus far.

I've been dreaming about death again. Old death so I know its new death. I dreamt about my mother. She was with a prominent prince. The father of the young prince that keep reminding me in my dreams that we are cousins - family. So I say unto him not because we share the same bloodline makes us family in my book. I know who my family is and it is with my good and true family that I stand in goodness and truth. That family is you Good God, my children and seeds – good seeds you've given me. The good family members that I know.

Onwards I go

Good God, I have never seen so much dutty clothes in a mi life. The house that my mother and prince was in was filled with dirty clothes. Even the toilet had dirty clothes in it. The dirty clothes reached the ceiling. Everywhere was dirty clothes. Wow.

Truly have mercy on my soul because I know my house needs cleaning. I have too much dirty laundry in my home hence I have to get them done.

I also dreamt my dead cousin Donald was talking to me but I cannot remember what he said. He was in black and his voice was of anger but he was not angry it was just the way he was talking.

I also dreamt about killing. I cannot fully remember the first half of the dream but the second half had to do with someone opening fire on a group of people.

Hence Good God woe be unto man.

I have to add this quickly because on the 23rd, I had this dream about QUICK LOOK. It had to do with phone servers and who is hacking and or using your phone server.

I know this morning (December 24, 2013) I was quarreling with you and I told you in 2014 I am going to walk away from you with my dignity because I do not want to go to hell and die for you or with you.

Evil is not my road Good God.

Pain is not my road and if I cannot walk truthfully in goodness and in truth including honesty and cleanliness with you, then it makes no sense for me to be with you.

It makes no sense that I write for you.

Like I've told you, you do not make me truly happy nor am I happy with you.

I've told you that it is not right for sin to cause humanity to go to hell and die. Hence on this day, December 24, 2013 if it be thy good and true will because it is my good and true will I infinitely and indefinitely with all the goodness of truth in me, curse the day Sin, Death, Satan, The Mother and Father of Sin and Evil and all that is evil was born. I truly curse that day because sin and the wickedness of sin have and has hurt all in humanity. So I truly curse them on this day and hope in goodness and in truth that you and all that is good exercise the law of death and that is "the wages of sin is death law."

All that is sinful and evil must now die because it is the law. Thus saith the Lord thy God meaning it is so.

Humanity – the good people – humans on this earth must now walk away from all that is sinful and evil.

The land and lands that commission the book of sin which is the book of the dead, the people that write the book of sin, the pastors, deacons, clergy that preach and teach from the book of sin, the bible and all the books of sin, the children of sin that carry out the works of sin, via unjust laws, death, selling of their souls to sin, the companies of sin, the financial institutions of sin and evil, the hospitals of sin and evil, the foundations of sin and evil, the people of sin and evil, the workers of sin and evil – all that is sinful, wicked and evil Good God, I curse infinitely and indefinitely on this day, December 24, 2013 for more than infinite and indefinite lifetimes and generations to come. All evil must be banished from earth, this universe.

Everywhere evil, sin, death and all the wickedness of sin and evil is must be banished to hell forever ever never to ever rise and return anywhere again.

So Good God no matter how sin use my mother to show me my family's bloodline.

No matter how this prince tries with his reminder of our family's bloodline, I cannot and will not go against you. I refuse to go against you because you told no one to commission the writing of the book of sin; which is the book of the dead. A book that kills people and bring their soul – spirit straight to hell. You deal in life, good life and not death. Hence I cannot in good faith or in good will plea for them.

Billions of people are going to lose their lives for what?

You don't send humanity to hell to die come on now. Life is given and you did give it to us good and true and because of this, good life; I eternally stand with you in all that is good and true forever ever.

Like I said, I know the hell you've taken me out of. I've lived it and I know the hell you are keeping me out of. I cannot in good faith go against you because when they were doing their ills none thought of the hurt and pain to you and humanity.

None thought of the hurt and pain earth herself would feel.

None thought about good and true life. I have to think of these things hence I hand sin's children over to death hence the curse of sin on the day of sin's birth and yes I curse the day sin was conceived as well.

You don't cause people to sin then hand them over to death like life does not matter. Good Life matters hence you are good life to me and forever ever will be.

I truly cannot stand against you because despite my ways and my pain you have been good to me.

Goodness is something that I will forever ever cherish. Hence I petition you for goodness and truth all the time.

I've told you leave sin's children as well as death's children alone because they are not for you. Sin destroys and sin have been trying to destroy you for a long time. My way is not of sin but of good life hence I truly cling to you.

Yes I too have sinned but I've come to and have made you my everything hence I do not fight for what's not mine. You are mine and like I told you, you are my right and no one has the right to come into my life and take you and your goodness from me.

I do not want or need what the devil and his children has. I need your goodness and truth hence I need your good wealth and prosperity. So no matter the family linkage I cannot in good faith nor can I in truth plea or plead for the ones who have hurt you and humanity. They aided the devil in destroying you and your children for profit – gain.

No I will not condemn the White Jews because that is your right. Hence I leave them to your storm and the hell that they've created for themselves literally. But if I could curse them and if I can, they too are cursed on this day, December 24, 2013. If I can't curse them then my actions will mean nothing. It will be null and void for the White Jews only because in truth Good God, their judgement belongs to you because they did sin against you.

They did aid the devil against you hence they're married to sin – the devil. Hence their six pointed star. The Star of Death or the Dead.

As for you It Things – Transgender It Things, you are already curse and on this day just to solidify the curse, I infinitely and indefinitely on this day, December 24, 2013 curse all of you and banish you all to hell infinitely and indefinitely. You don't change your sex and lie to people for them to become condemned like you.

As for the homosexual community that are being hypocrites, continue with your actions of hypocrisy and see if I don't petition Good God to make all of you a curse. Life is not a joke and you have to remember not everyone is going to like you. I've been through it so truly love you. Good God has not condemned you so truly do not condemn yourself or let me condemn you because I truly don't want to. But if I have to trust me I will. If someone do not like you do no hire them or bring them into your fold. If you are clean stay the hell away from unclean.

Do not tell anyone that they have to be homosexual or bi-sexual in order for them to have employment. You are infinitely and indefinitely wrong if you do so.

Trust me I am giving you a lifeline of hope so thread lightly and use your lifeline correctly. Like I said, Good God is not against you, you are the ones that are against you because you lock yourselves up in closets. Good God's doors have always been open so why close them and become closet or closed door people?

As for you Good God on this day, December 24, 2013, I truly and infinitely bless you with all that is good and true, clean and honest forever ever. Hold your head up in pride because you truly did good by me.

You are my true and good family hence I am a part of your lineage.

I am a part of your good and true family. So live in goodness and in truth because in all you've done for me you've done it in goodness and in truth.

I truly thank you for all.

As 2013 comes to a close hold on because despite me leaving you in 2014 I am clean because you did raise me right.

You did do good by me.

Yes my children have been through hell but you held on to them. You helped me with them in many ways and I truly thank you for that also.

I truly thank you for all the good help you have given me in my life no matter how small it was.

You did good because you did not raise a nasty or dirty child but a clean one with clean hands and a clean heart.

You taught me goodness and kindness hence truly bless South Africa – Sud, the lands of South Africa including Jamaica because I truly want and need the land of my birth to become clean but death must take his evil and wicked people. Also bless Kenya and China because of the goodness of Eva and Lucy.

Truly bless Scotland because that country is also a part of my ancestral home.

I so cannot forget them.

France and Russia, including Spain I leave to you. But I am hoping you will bless them too if they clean themselves up.

As for America hell no because I am thinking of their unjust laws, Tata and how they deemed him a terrorist.

Martin Luther King Jr. and how they killed him.

Marcus Mosiah Garvey and how they tainted him and instigated a witch hunt to destroy him and his character.

Robert Nesta Marley and how they murdered him by injecting him with cancer that killed him.

Oh yeah as for the racist whites of South Africa that tried to develop a drug to wipe all blacks off the face of the planet. Curse of curses infinitely and indefinitely be unto them all forever ever. Curse be unto you. Allelujah let thy will be done on this day, December 24, 2013 Good God. Have no mercy for them nor see with them for this.

As for Germany excluding Jamaican Germans duly remember the burning of the Flag of Life, Jamaican Flag. No I will not curse them but I truly leave them and Israel unto you because in their cases JUDGEMENT IS YOURS. Thus saith the Lord thy God meaning it is so. Woo Nelly because hell will have no fury like your fury when it comes to them.

And Good God if I have sinned in anyway against you and man for my cursing and asking on this day, December 24, 2013 truly forgive me infinitely and indefinitely for my sin and sins.

Michelle Jean

OTHER BOOKS BY MICHELLE JEAN

Blackman Redemption – The Fall of Michelle Jean
Blackman Redemption – After the Fall Apology
Blackman Redemption – World Cry – Christine Lewis
Blackman Redemption
Blackman Redemption – The Rise and Fall of Jamaica
Blackman Redemption – The War of Israel
Blackman Redemption – The Way I Speak to God
Blackman Redemption – A Little Talk With Man
Blackman Redemption – The Den of Thieves
Blackman Redemption – The Death of Jamaica
Blackman Redemption – Happy Mother's Day
Blackman Redemption – The Death of Faith
Blackman Redemption – The War of Religion
Blackman Redemption – The Death of Russia
Blackman Redemption – The Truth
Blackman Redemption – Spiritual War

The New Book of Life
The New Book of Life – A Cry For The Children
The New Book of Life – Judgement
The New Book of Life – Love Bound
The New Book of Life - Me

Just One of Those Days
Book Two – Just One of Those Days
Just One of Those Days – Book Three The Way I Feel
Just One of Those Days – Book Four

The Days I Am Weak
Crazy Thoughts – My Book of Sin
Broken

Ode to Mr. Dean Fraser

A Little Little Talk
A Little Little Talk – Book Two

Prayers
My Collective
A Little Talk/A Time For Fun and Play
Simple Poems
Behind The Scars
Songs of Praise And Love

Love Bound
Love Bound – Book Two

Dedication Unto My Kids
More Talk
Saving America From A Woman's Perspective
My Collective the Other Side of Me
My Collective the Dark Side of Me
A Blessed Day
Lose To Win
My Doubtful Days – Book One

My Little Talk With God
My Little Talk With God – Book Two

A Different Mood and World – Thinking

My Nagging Day
My Nagging Day – Book Two

Friday September 13, 2013
My True Love
It Would Be You
My Day